Cards for Gran

Explorer Challenge

What does Mum make
with this paper?

OXFORD
UNIVERSITY PRESS

Gran was in hospital.

She had a bad leg.

"We can make Gran get-well cards," said Chip.

"We can make pop-up cards," said Mum.

"Fold it and then cut it,"
said Mum.

"This bit will pop up," she said.

"This fan will pop up,"
said Chip.

"It is a pop-up Gran," said Chip.

Biff had a pop-up card.
"It is a cat," she said.

"Just the job," said Mum.

Kipper got a pen.

"This is a pop-up frog," he said.
"A frog?" said Mum.

"It is to tell Gran to hop up," said Kipper.

"Get well and get hopping, Gran," said Kipper.

"I cannot hop yet, Kipper,"
said Gran.

"Yes you can," said Kipper.
"Hop in, Gran."

Retell the Story

Look at the pictures and retell the story in your own words.

Look Back, Explorers

Why was Gran in hospital?

What was on the card that Chip made?

Imagine you are visiting Gran in hospital. What questions would you ask her?

Did you find out what Mum made with this paper?

Explorer Challenge: a flower (page 15)

What's Next, Explorers?

Now read about how you can make pop-up cards ...

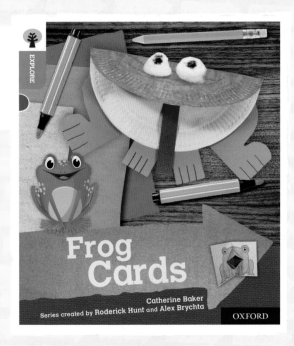

Explorer Challenge
for *Frog Cards*

What does this turn into?